ZRY
9/11

D1503756

WHALES SET I

SPERM WHALES

Megan M. Gunderson
ABDO Publishing Company

visit us at
www.abdopublishing.com

Published by ABDO Publishing Company, 8000 West 78th Street, Edina, Minnesota 55439.
Copyright © 2011 by Abdo Consulting Group, Inc. International copyrights reserved in all countries. No part of this book may be reproduced in any form without written permission from the publisher. The Checkerboard Library™ is a trademark and logo of ABDO Publishing Company.

Printed in the United States of America, North Mankato, Minnesota.
042010
092010

 PRINTED ON RECYCLED PAPER

Cover Photo: Alamy
Interior Photos: Alamy pp. 15, 19; Getty Images pp. 8, 21; National Geographic Stock p. 17; Peter Arnold p. 5; Photolibrary pp. 11, 13; Uko Gorter pp. 7, 9

Editor: Tamara L. Britton
Art Direction & Cover Design: Neil Klinepier

Library of Congress Cataloging-in-Publication Data

Gunderson, Megan M., 1981-
  Sperm whales / Megan M. Gunderson.
      p. cm. -- (Whales)
  Includes index.
  ISBN 978-1-61613-451-8
  1. Sperm whale--Juvenile literature. 2. Sperm whale. 3. Whales. I. Title.
QL737.C435G86 2011
  599.5'47--dc22
                              2010007283

CONTENTS

Sperm Whales and Family

Sperm whales are among the deepest diving whales on Earth. But, they must still surface to breathe! They take in air through a slit-like blowhole. It sits left of center near the tip of the snout. As mammals, these great whales are also **warm-blooded** and nurse their young with milk.

The sperm whale is named for the spermaceti **organ** that fills its huge head. The organ holds a liquid wax called spermaceti. A single sperm whale's head can contain 530 gallons (2,000 L) of this material!

The sperm whale has the largest brain of any mammal.

    These giant **cetaceans** share features with two much smaller relatives. These are the pygmy sperm whale and the dwarf sperm whale. However, sperm whales are the only members of their family, Physeteridae.

SHAPE, SIZE, AND COLOR

The sperm whale has a big, blocky head. In fact, its head makes up at least a quarter of its total body length! A long, narrow lower jaw opens under its large head.

The sperm whale's flippers are short and broad. On its back, there is a low dorsal hump. Behind that, a row of bumps called knuckles leads to triangular flukes.

Male sperm whales grow up to 62 feet (19 m) long. They usually weigh between 77,000 and 110,000 pounds (35,000 and 50,000 kg). Females are smaller. They reach about 40 feet (12 m) long and weigh much less.

BLOWHOLE

SPERM WHALE

EYE

FLIPPER

DORSAL
HUMP

KNUCKLES

Sperm whales have dark bluish gray or dusky gray brown skin. This wrinkly skin may also look black or pale brown. Most sperm whales have some white on their undersides. There is white around the mouth, too.

FLUKES

7

WHERE THEY LIVE

Before deep dives, sperm whales lift their flukes out of the water.

Sperm whales are found in every ocean on Earth. They like to live where **continental shelves** drop off to deep water. Sperm whales often swim in water that reaches 3,300 to 9,800 feet (1,000 to 3,000 m) deep.

Both male and female sperm whales **migrate**. But, their travel patterns are different. Females

Where Do Sperm Whales Live?

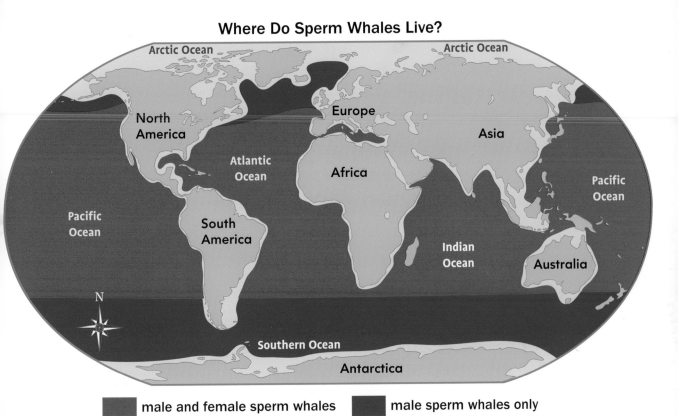

male and female sperm whales ■ male sperm whales only

stay within **tropical** and **temperate** waters. They move away from the **equator** in summer and toward it in winter.

Males range much farther. In summer, they may swim as far as Arctic or Antarctic waters. Males even travel between different ocean **basins**.

SENSES

Sperm whales look and listen above water by spyhopping. They bob their heads up to check out their surroundings. Sperm whales have keen eyesight and hearing underwater, too.

When underwater, sperm whales make very loud clicks. These clicks have several purposes, such as helping the whales find prey.

The spermaceti **organ** may help create and focus these sounds. When the sounds hit objects in a whale's path, they bounce back as echoes. The whale listens for these echoes. The sounds provide much information about the whale's surroundings. This process is called echolocation.

Sperm whales don't just rely on seeing and hearing. They also have well-developed senses of touch and taste. But, scientists do not think they have a sense of smell.

Sperm whales rely on keen senses to survive.

DEFENSE

Sperm whales have few natural enemies. Killer whales will attack them. However, scientists do not think those attacks succeed very often. Young sperm whales must also watch out for large sharks.

Adult female sperm whales work hard to protect their young from enemies. They will form a circle around the younger whales. They point their heads inward and their flukes out toward the danger.

Even with these dangers, humans are the sperm whale's greatest threat. They regularly hunted these whales from the early 1700s to the 1980s.

The sperm whale's body oil was used for lamp fuel and cosmetics. Oil from the spermaceti **organ** hardens to wax when exposed to air. It was used in candles and automobiles. Ambergris, a substance from the intestines, was used in making perfume.

Little hunting is allowed today, but human threats remain. Ship traffic is a concern because sperm whales may be struck by large boats. Or, they may accidentally become caught in fishing nets. Noise and water pollution are also harmful.

When chased, sperm whales swim up to 19 miles per hour (30 km/h).

FOOD

Sperm whales have big appetites! Every day, they eat up to 3 percent of their body weight. These hungry whales will eat octopuses, rays, sharks, and other fish. But their favorite food is squid. They dive deep to catch this delicious prey.

Sperm whales have up to 60 teeth in the lower jaw. These strong, cone-shaped teeth grow up to eight inches (20 cm) long. However, the whales don't seem to rely on them for catching prey. In fact, scientists have found healthy sperm whales that have no teeth at all!

The spermaceti **organ** is more important for hunting. It aids echolocation, which sperm whales use to find prey. And, it may help focus the loud sounds they make to stun prey!

Scientists are still studying how this **organ** helps sperm whales stay underwater longer. These whales dive thousands of feet down for more than two hours at a time. Deep below the surface, they stay still and wait for their prey.

Sperm whales have eaten squid up to 34 feet (10.5 m) long!

BABIES

Sperm whales usually mate in spring. A mother sperm whale is **pregnant** for up to 19 months. Then she gives birth to a single baby. It is called a calf. Calves are usually born in autumn.

Sperm whale calves are already 13 feet (4 m) long at birth. They weigh nearly 2,200 pounds (1,000 kg)! Usually, calves nurse for up to 42 months. But, some nurse off and on for as long as 13 years.

Female sperm whales keep growing until they are 28 years old. Males don't stop growing until age 35. Sperm whales can live as long as 77 years.

A mother sperm whale
waits three to six years
before having another calf.

17

BEHAVIORS

Sperm whales are social creatures. Thousands join together when **migrating**. The rest of the time, the whales form smaller groups. Adult females, younger whales, and calves often form schools of 20 to 40 individuals.

Adult males form groups of 12 to 15. But as they age and grow, those groups get smaller. Eventually, many older males become solitary.

Whether alone or in groups, sperm whales communicate with one another. Their whistles, squeaks, and other sounds can be heard for miles underwater.

Each whale also has its own group of clicks that it repeats. It uses these sounds when meeting other sperm whales. That is just one more amazing feature of these special sea creatures.

Sperm whales rest at the water's surface. This is called logging because they look like floating logs!

SPERM WHALE FACTS

Scientific Name: *Physeter macrocephalus*

Common Name: Sperm whale

Other Names: Cachalot, cachelot, pot whale, spermacet whale

Average Size:

Length – up to 62 feet (19 m) for males and 40 feet (12 m) for females

Weight – 77,000 to 110,000 pounds (35,000 to 50,000 kg) for males, but females weigh much less

Where They Are Found: In all oceans

The name macrocephalus is from a Greek word meaning "big head."

GLOSSARY

basin - a large area of Earth's surface covered by an ocean.

cetacean (sih-TAY-shuhn) - a member of the order Cetacea. Mammals such as dolphins, whales, and porpoises are cetaceans.

continental shelf - a shallow, underwater plain forming a continent's border. It ends with a steep slope to the deep ocean floor.

equator - an imaginary circle around the middle of Earth. It is halfway between the North and South poles.

migrate - to move from one place to another, often to find food.

organ - a part of an animal or a plant composed of several kinds of tissues. An organ performs a specific function. The heart, liver, gallbladder, and intestines are organs of an animal.

pregnant - having one or more babies growing within the body.

temperate - relating to an area where average temperatures range between 50 and 55 degrees Fahrenheit (10 and 13°C).

tropical - relating to an area with an average temperature above 77 degrees Fahrenheit (25°C) where no freezing occurs.

warm-blooded - having a body temperature that is not much affected by surrounding air or water.

WEB SITES

To learn more about sperm whales, visit ABDO Publishing Company on the World Wide Web at **www.abdopublishing.com**. Web sites about sperm whales are featured on our Book Links page. These links are routinely monitored and updated to provide the most current information available.

INDEX